Hard Some

Hailey Higdon

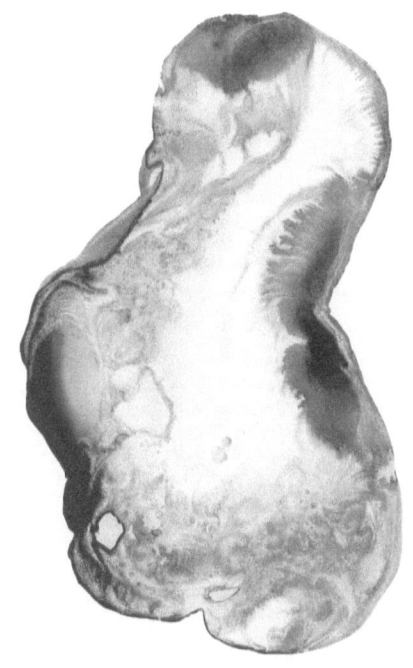

Spuyten Duyvil
New York City

© 2019 Hailey Higdon

ISBN 978-1-947980-97-6

Library of Congress Cataloging-in-Publication Data

Names: Higdon, Hailey, author.
Title: Hard some / Hailey Higdon.
Description: New York City : Spuyten Duyvil, [2019]
Identifiers: LCCN 2018045032 | ISBN 9781947980976
Subjects: LCSH: American poetry--21st century.
Classification: LCC PS3608.I355+ | DDC 811/.6--dc23
LC record available at https://lccn.loc.gov/2018045032

Life being an unbroken motion of consciousness,
poetry is for me the celebration of that unbrokenness.

—Will Alexander, *from* "My Interior Vita"

A Wild Permanence

Two women walk into a town.

two women walk into a town
so here we are digging, digging
until we're wild, find water   all of the places were open
then they were closed   what kind of reception you get
you get, so the sun is gathering bystanders
perfectly, like there is no harm

everywhere I go

they are waiting   as an American I want to talk about myself

go in and out of getting prayer, suggest light

exposure   about myself, I spoiled with competition

a country so green we all wanted it

then to have that particular experience of being talked

out of the conversation

two women walk into a town
good   we tried for neighborly
in the shadow of a repeated national harm, shit-show
destroyed towns, big and small people
violence used in relation to purity
some in a boat and others wondering how long
it will take to sink the middle, which is terrible

two women go to places inhabited by risk, no job
too odd   there are real time moments before death
when real gets real
the rest is made up, costumed
we are out to eat, sampling the buffet
looking to see what's in the garbage can
because we are young and curious and just want to know

the fear of the dark is the fear
of making out, making it   we didn't know what
we were doing   we were trying, showing   some people
surface, they figure it out
between us evaporates, chisels out one form   they didn't expect
two to be there

two women walk into a town, foundational
to the existence of the town as interesting
they thought　　　　　we need the witness
of neighbors　　　　　we don't know
who are neighbors, who
are just friends　　　　here is not a place for inside behavior, but outside
doesn't seem
much better

what comes next?   two women talked awhile
while the world was changing   weather
screamed in the evening that it wasn't enough
to decide how you feel independent of your neighbors
did it matter if they agreed?   we are here, permanent & wild with
that community of moving target, that community
that says you are better off real imaginary and real far away

so today say we built a house out of brick
say they huffed and they puffed
they are powerful, find
complacency easy
so why did we build this house out of brick?   and why
did they huff and they puff?
the thunder counsels the lightening strike then shuts up
now it is Monday and expandable and expanding we roam we roam
so day we roam, submissive to the course

two women walk into a town, busted
up like they've been somewhere
leaning into the shadow of subtle, responsible
captioning the night
two women atmospheric
all the love of loving a new place
but told to count their blessings
that living is consent to dying after

we turn out the lights

sit in the back of the truck and look at the darkness of woods

we call polite moments moments of rescue

when our community momentarily becomes our community

but we bloom at variance

because we are always thinking, you say

about ways to get better at being the most *you* version of *you*

you know they don't like

right?   people are
seeds leaving you
until you acknowledge they
were grafted too   two women sew rest
the times we should have had
squandered time on the internet, hiding, trying to figure
things out

no no no the way it is is we have trouble anticipating
failures   our neighbors didn't know how it would
turn out so they pretended
pretending was consent   we think hum…
doesn't feel right, fair   what's a life without choices?
that free person each day he bought an ice cream cone, thought about
swimming   made volitional acts
when he woke up, went somewhere

we agree to be on water
swimming at our own risk
this is how my birthday
is going to be, she says   I did
some things, too busy for others   what do
you care?

I hear it is a tough topic, they say   a woman needs
a seed   we moved to the farthest place
where company is the slow bouncing of tree limbs
where the jitter of leaves nowadays is symbolic
two women walk into a desert town
there is not so much of an audience but
suggestion of exposure, light

then we are there   there

to feel the pressure of exclusion, which can be

a fuel, familiar

if terrible, if the prototype of queer is determinate

two women try to remind themselves

the safety of having a regular job or

a corner store

light falls on the floor in the quiet room
there's every day at the lake
every day we took care of each other
and it was masculine and it was feminine
wearing the same clothes like it was making us
more ourselves

we are scuffmarks on floorboards
a wild permanence
looks like crystal, behavior that is not a threat to common values
but remarkable in its individual means
who we need is a ball change in the movement of walking
full of exceptions
no matter the rules I break

no matter

they will

domesticate me after I die

the ratio of men to you   and well and

and those were the reasons, and that was new york

BREAKER

Fuck the lake.

fuck the lake I split into
the sea   most
relationships I've had I've
been you

a fan

a hem, a toehold   the place where
a creature and its shadow are connected
that way love is
tunneled
to know you, of relief
of latching to another person

ask me about   yes, your life
when I look at you on the bed in the dark you're perfect
open in different combinations of the same set   accepting
both done and undone
from its nucleus to its bounds
its bounds to its nucleus
not afraid of the symbolic   the representation of joy
and its many undone expressions

how many times do we try something new
and before it feels comfortable   retaliate

things we take turns enjoying
never quite experience together
you are too close to the information you carry
but you carry it because there is comfort
in co-experience
conditioning, habituation
keeping the things that expect reiteration

how does the old story go?
I started to hold the sea accountable for backing off
to ask it to come closer
it is good to be near
more than abbreviations   some difficult
some big
I started seeing big   in shifts
half day half night   aware
sometimes not a good person

things get better   boundaries form
the boys queue up at the diving board
the outline of their trunks as they flip off
into the silver gloss of the lake
on the rope that marks the swimming area, boys hold on
heads bobbing like buoys

the boys last long on the lake
the fog lasts long on the sea
fuck the lake its perfect doughy
edges   I went to the world and found you buried in me
the great   unwashed
patched   mascots for me to love

fuck the lake

I got angry   yellow

you a spotlight   tracked a performance

we take turns enjoying

but never quite experience together

now look see

I've been into myself too

the way I own my own headache   I was done living
that way, dependable with complaint   I knew everything
except how to live without complement
but there was privacy in not having to be fully myself all the time
where someone
crashes near me I crash too
fuck the lake
fuck the lake

I come across   blue milestones
but never make it
to the other side
in with the wide wide sea
I am the wide wide sea
breaker   seeing you again
tossing ideas around
what the fuck is domestic
suffering?

I imagined vulnerability was liability
unproductive, inconvenient
I dreamed about responsibility, losing
how did the story go?
I leave with the big, big sea's
big seams   tossed around

oh boat I made
where wreck is a good thing and death opens little doors
big break me   the ocean's teeth
knock in the night and never stop
that same old magic   a body calibrates
pretending to be nonchalant

CHILDREN

Some run.

some children take their authority from death

some run

what do you care

about pipes and seven thirty

it's always 7:30

tell me something good

everyone is your mother

some run
retaliate
and labor
labor
which is repressed anger
at the world of problems
some run
out the role of a sable
some just take take take
take take take

had your body floated
paddle quick before now
had wrenches
sunk the basement
had mission
had children
had I met a framer

hand wrung by design
in some other neighborhood
repeat after me:
> learning is an act
> not learning is an act
> yesterday is woolly
> leading on you
> leading you on
> leading on you

children
what happened
when you
were young
give
the good
news first

btw what living

things need

is to no longer need

then they wouldn't

be living

no longer

btw how you treat you

is reciprocal

because you are more than one

things happen

in pairs

and define each other

some children

some run

some

some run chicken

some left behind

some run
come run
come run, look
a vision not yet change tolerant
put on your coat
what is coming, come quick
ask me about my day

it's a fail-safe

to leak beyond your own creation

not anticipating the color

or spiritual act

those were

the conditions

you were the rainbow

it was impermanent

a gulf
let it go fraud in the relationship
and furnished
when it's finished
with you

rainbows take their authority from death
put the good stuff back in the system
forgivable
it's forgivable
you don't miss anything
child have child
have missions
with permission to blow things up

some run

shop, score, station

pay obeisance

some place to be safe

some place to be safe

what don't kill you don't make you

do no harm or
give gratitude
find insurance
how to carry a piano bench and
reach to grab a rosemary bush
after the parade

see my relationship to you is you, wild thing

see you're going to get everybody barking

some run one to another
how do you do
2 things with a person
who does nothing for you

some run

company

cleaning the same thing together

trying to make everything perfect in the apartment for everyone

the floorboards ask you to step lighter

you go

some run

I was told to let it come and go
some run
a privilege
no person saw an image
no child said one thing but meant the opposite

there is no need / work
fruit / flowers
land some
ask:
How is this person a mirror?
turn into another
you trafficked by potential, still awed by
excavation
children
some run, work and work free
to be the best to you

Yes & What Happens

I believe we come back.

here's what it is: I say *yes* a lot
go wide, not deep, what happens
when we agree to duty, deals, what happens when we die?
where the best you for you
is melting into your instrument
is drawing you closer to being one thing

to meet you for dinner is recommending
defeat, a shared plate, giving something up
I haven't the vacuum-packed counsel of my friends
their opinions pour into a backyard
assumption that I am unalterable (yes) shooting off events (yes) patterned
to find the trouble in union

that time I was angry for more typical reasons
at my mother, or wanting to remain steely, effortful
I saw a picture of the Salton Sea
crusted in all directions
what thirsty ways I've tried to out fox
the books about softening

to believe in process, in moment to moment, to let
to be as queer as you are without boundaries
the giving part, man, how do you do it?
you go like everyone else
you go through it
not under, not around

for flavor I drove to the city
reaching into the pocket of the evening to encounter both closeness
and far away, asking
this much more of my instrument, I believe we come
back, I believe we come back like fashion, used cars
pedestrians give in to, the dark intersections of the city
connecting with the man who sat in front of me twice

my version of care is unaccustomed to temperate weather
a product of false advertising
in the silence of a sick day I am grateful for the extra hour
the opportunity to track you
be in the canoe and not paddle
I had a dream of melting into other people

and other conventional things

I lugged solitude from place to place

I lugged trees across trampolines, kindness across violence

I believe we come back

angling new experiences like short cuts, quick starts

I believe we come back, shoulder standing for better views

I believe the mind is an aquarium, a holding tank
boats part the Snohomish River, loud mothers like motorcycles
it came from a sad place all that wronging
all that doing it to someone else
then the idea that we can co-mingle
by bond and not just biology

revealing the colonization of our cognitive processes
I believe we come back, back when we were
without compression, interacting more like an amalgam
doing things better
how reciprocity is our first form of influence
how you were taught the river, its curves, its dry spots

when I'm lonely I go to the drug store
look at the clearance bins
there are people waiting to be loved, love sick
there are open spaces, what happens
what happened in the flood?
I believe we come back, thank you

the rivers of the world became the sea and they
were also rivers, tied to each individual place
that dream of revealing, not caring about too much
that dream of fixing other people
that dream where everything that is neglected speaks to power
that dream in which I predicted violence

that dream where you escape
I went to the drug store when I was lonely
I was looking for souls that were older than mine
what happens, what happens when you die
that dream where you escape
experience, turn up older anyway

thank you for waiting, incurring the damages
which were going to happen, I've been told
everything was always going to happen, and
away from you and near you are the same thing, and
it was Sunday, and I did laundry, and you were all there
all my changes, all my changes were there

Acknowledgments & Thanks

The last lines of these four poems, in order of appearance, come from the music of Leonard Cohen, Patty Griffin, Blood Orange, and Neil Young. Their single strings tied up the nativity of a new way of seeing myself as a poet. I am so grateful for them.

Cover art by Sara Schneckloth. This piece is a part of a larger collection of Breathing Stones that Schneckloth created and animated. You can participate with these stones by going to https://breathingstones.com/. You can find more of Schneckloth's work at http://www.saraschneckloth.com/.

A Wild Permanence was originally published as a chapbook by Dancing Girl Press. Thank you to Kristy Bowen, a relentless champion of women in poetry.

Yes & What Happens was originally published in a limited edition as a part of the Dusie Kollektiv.

Thank you to Wellspring House and Sundress Academy of the Arts for generous support to create portions of this work.

The phrase "fuck the lake" comes from a letter Joan Mitchell wrote to Michael Goldberg in 1954. More of the letter reads, "fuck the lake—and fuck my reactions to it and the past—shit it's depressing." As my friends will know, my family has a close connection to Joan. My aunt, Phyllis Hailey, was an astonishing artist who lived and painted with Joan in Vétheuil. Phyllis died in a car crash in France shortly before I was born, and I bear her name, Phyllis Hailey Higdon. Though only a slim number of people call me "Phil" anymore.

Thank you to Sara Schneckloth for your solidarity and beautiful work. Thank you also to the friends who have shown confidence in me and this work, even if we don't talk enough: Dolly Garay, Lyllyan Blare (and M'Liyah), Lewis Freedman, Nicole Donnelly, Sarah Heady, Maged Zaher, David Shalen and many other old and new friends. I love you all.

Thank you to my family—Mom, Dad, Patrick, Grace and baby Phee.

Finally, thank you to Tanya, for everything.

HAILEY HIGDON is a poet from Nashville. She is the author of several chapbooks including *A Wild Permanence* (Dancing Girl, 2018), *Rural* (Drop Leaf, 2017), *The State in Which* (Above/Ground, 2013), *Packing* (Bloof Books, 2012) and *How to Grow Almost Everything* (Agnes Fox, 2011). *Hard Some* is her first full-length collection. She currently lives and works in Seattle.

Find her online at haileyhaileyhailey.com.

www.ingramcontent.com/pod-product-compliance
Lightning Source LLC
Chambersburg PA
CBHW020127130526
44591CB00032B/559